EMMANUEL JOSEPH

The Pinnacle of Unity, Fusing Personal Development with Financial and Relational Prosperity

Copyright © 2025 by Emmanuel Joseph

All rights reserved. No part of this publication may be reproduced, stored or transmitted in any form or by any means, electronic, mechanical, photocopying, recording, scanning, or otherwise without written permission from the publisher. It is illegal to copy this book, post it to a website, or distribute it by any other means without permission.

First edition

This book was professionally typeset on Reedsy. Find out more at reedsy.com

Contents

1. Chapter 1: The Foundation of Self-Awareness — 1
2. Chapter 2: Goal Setting: The Roadmap to Success — 3
3. Chapter 3: Embracing a Growth Mindset — 5
4. Chapter 4: Financial Literacy: The Bedrock of Prosperity — 7
5. Chapter 5: The Psychology of Money — 9
6. Chapter 6: Building Wealth Through Smart Investing — 11
7. Chapter 7: The Importance of Financial Planning — 13
8. Chapter 8: The Power of Connection — 15
9. Chapter 9: Strengthening Family Bonds — 17
10. Chapter 10: Building a Strong Social Network — 19
11. Chapter 11: The Role of Emotional Intelligence — 21
12. Chapter 12: Work-Life Balance: Achieving Harmony — 23
13. Chapter 13: Cultivating Gratitude and Positivity — 25
14. Chapter 14: The Synergy of Personal Development, Financial... — 27
15. Chapter 15: The Journey to the Pinnacle of Unity — 29

1

Chapter 1: The Foundation of Self-Awareness

Personal development begins with a deep understanding of oneself. **Self-awareness is the cornerstone of growth, providing clarity on strengths, weaknesses, and aspirations.** When individuals take the time to understand their inner worlds, they can make more informed decisions, set meaningful goals, and live authentically.

One effective technique for cultivating self-awareness is mindfulness practice. Mindfulness involves paying attention to the present moment without judgment. It allows individuals to observe their thoughts and emotions as they arise, providing valuable insights into their inner landscapes. Regular mindfulness practice can help individuals become more attuned to their reactions, patterns, and triggers, leading to greater self-understanding.

Another powerful tool for developing self-awareness is journaling. Writing down thoughts, feelings, and experiences can help individuals process and reflect on their lives. Journaling provides a safe space to explore inner conflicts, uncover hidden desires, and track personal growth. By regularly reviewing journal entries, individuals can gain a deeper understanding of their journeys and identify areas for improvement.

Seeking feedback from others is also essential for building self-awareness. **Honest feedback from trusted friends, family members, or colleagues**

can offer new perspectives and reveal blind spots. Constructive criticism helps individuals recognize their strengths and areas for growth. Actively listening to feedback and reflecting on it can lead to significant personal development.

In summary, self-awareness is the foundation upon which personal growth is built. By practicing mindfulness, journaling, and seeking feedback, individuals can gain a deeper understanding of themselves. This self-awareness serves as a guiding light, illuminating the path to a fulfilling and authentic life.

2

Chapter 2: Goal Setting: The Roadmap to Success

Effective goal setting transforms dreams into achievable milestones. **Setting clear and well-defined goals provides direction, motivation, and a sense of purpose.** Without goals, individuals may feel lost or aimless, lacking the focus needed to achieve their aspirations.

One popular framework for goal setting is the SMART criteria. SMART goals are Specific, Measurable, Achievable, Relevant, and Time-bound. Specific goals are clear and unambiguous, outlining precisely what needs to be accomplished. Measurable goals include criteria to track progress and determine success. Achievable goals are realistic and attainable within the individual's capabilities. Relevant goals align with the individual's values and long-term objectives. Time-bound goals have deadlines, creating a sense of urgency and accountability.

Visualization is a powerful technique to enhance goal attainment. By vividly imagining the successful achievement of a goal, individuals can create a mental blueprint for success. Visualization helps build confidence, reduce anxiety, and reinforce the commitment to the goal. Combining visualization with positive affirmations can further strengthen the belief in one's ability to achieve the desired outcome.

Breaking down long-term goals into smaller, manageable steps is essential for maintaining motivation and tracking progress. **Each step serves as a mini-milestone, providing a sense of accomplishment and momentum.** Creating a detailed action plan with specific tasks and deadlines helps individuals stay organized and focused on their goals.

In conclusion, effective goal setting is the roadmap to success. By setting SMART goals, practicing visualization, and breaking down long-term objectives into manageable steps, individuals can turn their dreams into reality. **Goal setting provides the direction, motivation, and structure needed to achieve personal and professional aspirations.**

3

Chapter 3: Embracing a Growth Mindset

A growth mindset is the belief that abilities and intelligence can be developed through dedication and hard work. **This mindset fosters resilience, adaptability, and a love of learning.** Embracing a growth mindset can transform how individuals approach challenges and view their potential.

Carol Dweck, a renowned psychologist, introduced the concept of a growth mindset in her research. According to Dweck, individuals with a growth mindset see challenges as opportunities to learn and grow. They view failures as valuable learning experiences rather than as reflections of their abilities. This perspective encourages perseverance and a willingness to take on new and difficult tasks.

One way to cultivate a growth mindset is to reframe negative thoughts and self-talk. **When faced with a challenge, individuals can replace self-defeating thoughts like "I can't do this" with empowering statements like "I can learn how to do this."** This shift in perspective helps build confidence and resilience. Practicing self-compassion and acknowledging efforts and progress, rather than focusing solely on outcomes, also supports a growth mindset.

Another strategy is to embrace the learning process. Individuals with a growth mindset are open to feedback and eager to improve. Seeking opportunities for learning and development, such as taking courses, reading books, or attending workshops, fosters a love of learning. Celebrating small successes and progress along the way reinforces the belief in one's ability to grow and develop.

In summary, embracing a growth mindset can have a profound impact on personal and professional development. **By reframing negative thoughts, embracing the learning process, and viewing challenges as opportunities, individuals can cultivate resilience, adaptability, and a love of learning.** A growth mindset empowers individuals to reach their full potential and achieve their goals.

4

Chapter 4: Financial Literacy: The Bedrock of Prosperity

Financial literacy is essential for making informed decisions and building wealth. **Understanding the basics of money management empowers individuals to take control of their financial future.** Financial literacy involves knowledge of budgeting, saving, investing, and managing debt.

Budgeting is the foundation of financial literacy. **Creating a budget helps individuals track their income and expenses, identify spending patterns, and allocate resources effectively.** A well-planned budget ensures that essential needs are met, savings goals are achieved, and discretionary spending is controlled. Budgeting tools and apps can simplify the process and provide insights into financial habits.

Saving is a crucial aspect of financial stability and prosperity. **Building an emergency fund provides a financial safety net for unexpected expenses.** Setting aside a portion of income for savings helps individuals achieve short-term and long-term financial goals. Automatic savings plans can make saving easier and more consistent.

Investing is a powerful tool for wealth building. **Understanding different investment options, such as stocks, bonds, mutual funds, and real estate, allows individuals to grow their wealth over time.** Diversification, risk management, and long-term planning are key principles of successful investing. Educating oneself about investment strategies and seeking advice from financial professionals can enhance investment decisions.

Managing debt is another critical component of financial literacy. **Understanding the terms and conditions of loans, credit cards, and other forms of debt is essential for avoiding financial pitfalls.** Developing a repayment plan and prioritizing high-interest debt can help individuals reduce their debt burden and improve their financial health.

In conclusion, financial literacy is the bedrock of prosperity. By mastering the basics of budgeting, saving, investing, and managing debt, individuals can make informed decisions and build a secure financial future. **Financial literacy empowers individuals to achieve their financial goals and create a foundation for long-term prosperity.**

5

Chapter 5: The Psychology of Money

Money is not just a medium of exchange; it is intertwined with emotions and beliefs. **Understanding the psychological aspects of money can help individuals develop healthier financial habits.** This chapter delves into money scripts, spending habits, and financial stress, providing insights into the emotional and cognitive factors that influence financial behavior.

Money scripts are unconscious beliefs about money formed during childhood. These beliefs can shape spending and saving habits, often without individuals realizing it. Common money scripts include ideas like "money is the root of all evil" or "more money will make me happier." By identifying and challenging these scripts, individuals can develop a healthier relationship with money.

Spending habits are often influenced by emotional triggers. **Retail therapy, or shopping to alleviate stress or sadness, is a common example of emotional spending.** Recognizing the emotional factors that drive spending can help individuals make more conscious and intentional financial decisions. Techniques such as mindfulness and cognitive-behavioral therapy (CBT) can be effective in addressing emotional spending.

Financial stress is another important aspect of the psychology of money. **Worrying about money can take a toll on mental and physical health.** Strategies for managing financial stress include creating a budget, setting financial goals, and seeking support from a financial advisor. Practicing self-care and stress-reduction techniques, such as exercise and meditation, can also help alleviate financial anxiety.

In conclusion, understanding the psychology of money is essential for developing healthier financial habits. By recognizing money scripts, addressing emotional spending, and managing financial stress, individuals can improve their financial well-being. **Cultivating a healthy relationship with money is a key component of overall prosperity.**

6

Chapter 6: Building Wealth Through Smart Investing

Investing is a powerful tool for building wealth and achieving financial independence. **This chapter introduces various investment options and the principles of successful investing.** Understanding the basics of investing empowers individuals to make informed decisions and grow their wealth over time.

Stocks, bonds, mutual funds, and real estate are common investment options. **Each option has its own risk and return profile, making it important to diversify investments.** Diversification involves spreading investments across different asset classes to reduce risk. By balancing high-risk, high-reward investments with more stable options, individuals can achieve a well-rounded portfolio.

Risk management is a crucial aspect of investing. **Understanding risk tolerance and setting realistic investment goals can help individuals make informed decisions.** Long-term planning and patience are key to successful investing. Market fluctuations are normal, and maintaining a long-term perspective can help individuals stay focused on their goals.

Investing in education is another important aspect of building wealth. **Continuously learning about investment strategies, market trends, and financial planning can enhance decision-making.** Seeking advice from financial professionals and leveraging technology, such as investment apps and online resources, can also provide valuable insights and tools for successful investing.

In summary, smart investing is a powerful tool for building wealth. **By understanding investment options, diversifying investments, managing risk, and investing in education, individuals can achieve financial independence and long-term prosperity.** Successful investing requires patience, discipline, and a commitment to continuous learning.

7

Chapter 7: The Importance of Financial Planning

A comprehensive financial plan is a roadmap to achieving financial goals. **This chapter outlines the steps involved in creating a financial plan and the benefits of having a clear financial strategy.** Financial planning provides structure, clarity, and peace of mind, helping individuals navigate their financial journeys with confidence.

The first step in financial planning is assessing the current financial situation. **This involves reviewing income, expenses, assets, and liabilities to understand the financial landscape.** Creating a detailed financial snapshot provides a baseline for setting goals and developing strategies.

Setting financial goals is the next step. **Goals can be short-term, such as saving for a vacation, or long-term, such as planning for retirement.** Clearly defined goals provide direction and motivation, making it easier to develop actionable strategies. SMART criteria can be applied to financial goals to ensure they are Specific, Measurable, Achievable, Relevant, and Time-bound.

Developing strategies to achieve financial goals is a key component of financial planning. **This may include creating a budget, establishing savings plans, and exploring investment options.** Financial planning also involves risk management, such as having insurance and an emergency fund. Regularly reviewing and adjusting the financial plan ensures it remains aligned with changing circumstances and goals.

In conclusion, financial planning is essential for achieving financial goals and building a secure future. **By assessing the current financial situation, setting goals, and developing strategies, individuals can create a comprehensive financial plan that provides clarity and peace of mind.** Financial planning empowers individuals to take control of their financial journeys and achieve long-term prosperity.

8

Chapter 8: The Power of Connection

Human connections are fundamental to happiness and fulfillment. **Building and maintaining meaningful relationships enhances well-being and provides emotional support.** This chapter explores the importance of social connections and offers practical tips for nurturing relationships.

Social support has a significant impact on mental and physical health. **Strong relationships provide a sense of belonging, reduce stress, and increase resilience.** Social connections can come from various sources, including family, friends, colleagues, and community groups. Building a diverse social network enriches life and offers opportunities for personal and professional growth.

Active listening is a key skill for nurturing relationships. **Listening with empathy and without judgment fosters trust and understanding.** Being present and fully engaged in conversations shows respect and appreciation for others. Effective communication involves both speaking and listening, ensuring that both parties feel heard and valued.

Empathy is another important aspect of meaningful connections. **Understanding and sharing the feelings of others strengthen emotional bonds.** Practicing empathy involves putting oneself in another's shoes and responding with compassion. Acts of kindness, support, and encouragement further deepen connections and create a positive social environment.

In summary, the power of connection lies in building and maintaining meaningful relationships. **Social support, active listening, and empathy enhance well-being and provide emotional support.** Nurturing relationships enriches life and contributes to happiness and fulfillment. Investing in social connections is an essential aspect of personal and relational prosperity.

9

Chapter 9: Strengthening Family Bonds

Family is often the cornerstone of one's social network. **Strong family bonds provide emotional support, a sense of belonging, and a foundation for personal growth.** This chapter explores strategies for strengthening family bonds and creating a supportive family environment.

Creating traditions and rituals is a powerful way to strengthen family bonds. **Traditions, whether big or small, provide a sense of continuity and shared identity.** They create lasting memories and reinforce the connection between family members. Simple rituals, like family dinners or weekend outings, can have a significant impact on family cohesion.

Spending quality time together is essential for building strong family relationships. **Engaging in activities that everyone enjoys fosters connection and creates opportunities for meaningful interactions.** Whether it's playing games, going on trips, or simply having heartfelt conversations, quality time strengthens the emotional bonds within the family.

Effective communication is key to resolving conflicts and building understanding. **Open and honest communication fosters trust and prevents misunderstandings.** Encouraging family members to express their feelings and listen to each other with empathy creates a supportive environment. Conflict resolution techniques, such as active listening and finding common ground, can help address disagreements constructively.

In summary, strengthening family bonds involves creating traditions, spending quality time together, and fostering effective communication. **A supportive family environment enhances personal growth, well-being, and happiness.** Investing in family relationships is a crucial aspect of relational prosperity.

10

Chapter 10: Building a Strong Social Network

A diverse and robust social network provides emotional support, opportunities, and a sense of belonging. **Building and maintaining connections enriches life and offers numerous benefits.** This chapter discusses the importance of a strong social network and offers practical advice for expanding and nurturing connections.

A strong social network offers emotional support during challenging times. **Friends, colleagues, and community members provide encouragement, advice, and companionship.** Social connections create a sense of belonging and reduce feelings of loneliness. Building a diverse network with people from different backgrounds and experiences broadens perspectives and enriches life.

Networking is essential for personal and professional growth. **Building connections with like-minded individuals can lead to new opportunities, collaborations, and mentorship.** Attending social events, joining clubs or organizations, and participating in community activities are effective ways to expand one's social network. Developing genuine and meaningful relationships rather than superficial connections is key to building a strong network.

Overcoming social anxiety is important for building and maintaining connections. **Practicing social skills, setting realistic goals, and gradually exposing oneself to social situations can help reduce anxiety.** Seeking support from a therapist or joining social skills groups can also be beneficial. Building confidence in social interactions enhances the ability to connect with others.

In conclusion, building a strong social network provides emotional support, opportunities, and a sense of belonging. **Networking, overcoming social anxiety, and nurturing genuine relationships are essential for personal and professional growth.** Investing in social connections enhances well-being and contributes to a fulfilling and prosperous life.

11

Chapter 11: The Role of Emotional Intelligence

Emotional intelligence is the ability to recognize, understand, and manage one's own emotions and the emotions of others. **High emotional intelligence enhances relationships, communication, and personal growth.** This chapter explores the components of emotional intelligence and offers strategies for developing this essential skill.

Self-awareness is the foundation of emotional intelligence. **Recognizing and understanding one's own emotions is crucial for effective self-management.** Mindfulness practices, such as meditation and reflection, can help individuals become more attuned to their emotional states. Self-awareness allows individuals to respond to situations thoughtfully rather than react impulsively.

Self-regulation involves managing emotions in a healthy and constructive manner. **Techniques such as deep breathing, positive self-talk, and problem-solving can help individuals regulate their emotions.** Developing self-regulation skills enhances resilience and reduces stress. It allows individuals to navigate challenges with a calm and composed mindset.

Empathy is the ability to understand and share the feelings of others. **Practicing empathy strengthens relationships and fosters connection.** Active listening, putting oneself in another's shoes, and responding with compassion are key aspects of empathy. Developing empathy enhances social interactions and creates a supportive and understanding environment.

Social skills are another important component of emotional intelligence. **Effective communication, conflict resolution, and collaboration skills enhance relationships and teamwork.** Practicing assertiveness, active listening, and non-verbal communication techniques can improve social interactions. Building strong social skills contributes to personal and professional success.

In summary, emotional intelligence enhances relationships, communication, and personal growth. **Developing self-awareness, self-regulation, empathy, and social skills are essential for high emotional intelligence.** Investing in emotional intelligence enhances well-being and contributes to a fulfilling and prosperous life.

12

Chapter 12: Work-Life Balance: Achieving Harmony

Achieving a balance between work and personal life is essential for overall well-being. **Work-life balance enhances happiness, productivity, and personal fulfillment.** This chapter explores the challenges of work-life balance and offers strategies for managing time and energy effectively.

Setting boundaries between work and personal life is crucial for maintaining balance. **Defining clear work hours and personal time helps prevent burnout and ensures that both work and personal needs are met.** Communicating boundaries with colleagues and family members creates mutual understanding and respect. Prioritizing self-care and personal activities enhances well-being and productivity.

Effective time management is key to achieving work-life balance. **Creating a schedule that includes both work tasks and personal activities helps individuals stay organized and focused.** Prioritizing tasks, delegating responsibilities, and avoiding multitasking can improve efficiency. Time management tools and techniques, such as to-do lists and time blocking, can simplify the process.

Self-care is an essential aspect of work-life balance. **Taking time for activities that nourish the body, mind, and soul enhances overall well-**

being. Regular exercise, healthy eating, and sufficient sleep are fundamental for physical health. Engaging in hobbies, spending time with loved ones, and practicing relaxation techniques support mental and emotional health.

Seeking support from others is important for maintaining work-life balance. **Talking to friends, family, or a therapist can provide valuable insights and encouragement.** Asking for help with responsibilities and sharing the load with others can reduce stress and create a sense of community. Building a support network enhances resilience and well-being.

In conclusion, achieving work-life balance is essential for overall well-being. **Setting boundaries, managing time effectively, prioritizing self-care, and seeking support are key strategies for maintaining balance.** Work-life balance enhances happiness, productivity, and personal fulfillment, contributing to a harmonious and prosperous life.

13

Chapter 13: Cultivating Gratitude and Positivity

Gratitude and positivity are powerful forces that enhance well-being and relationships. **Cultivating gratitude and a positive mindset can transform how individuals experience life.** This chapter explores the science behind gratitude and positivity, offering practical techniques for fostering these qualities.

Gratitude involves recognizing and appreciating the good things in life. **Keeping a gratitude journal is a simple yet effective practice for cultivating gratitude.** By regularly writing down things they are thankful for, individuals can shift their focus from what is lacking to what is abundant. This practice enhances overall happiness and provides a sense of contentment.

Acts of kindness are another way to cultivate gratitude and positivity. **Helping others, whether through small gestures or significant contributions, creates a sense of purpose and connection.** Acts of kindness can range from volunteering to offering a kind word to a stranger. These actions not only benefit others but also enhance the well-being of the giver.

A positive mindset involves focusing on the good aspects of situations and maintaining an optimistic outlook. **Practicing positive self-talk and challenging negative thoughts can help individuals develop a positive mindset.** Techniques such as visualization, affirmation, and mindfulness can also support a positive perspective. Embracing positivity enhances resilience and the ability to navigate challenges.

In summary, cultivating gratitude and positivity enhances well-being and relationships. **Practices such as keeping a gratitude journal, performing acts of kindness, and developing a positive mindset transform how individuals experience life.** Embracing gratitude and positivity fosters happiness, resilience, and a sense of fulfillment.

14

Chapter 14: The Synergy of Personal Development, Financial Prosperity, and Relationships

Personal development, financial prosperity, and meaningful relationships are interconnected and mutually reinforcing. **Achieving harmony between these pillars contributes to a fulfilling and prosperous life.** This chapter explores the synergy between personal growth, financial planning, and relationship-building.

Personal development provides the foundation for financial and relational prosperity. **Self-awareness, goal setting, and a growth mindset enhance the ability to achieve financial goals and build meaningful relationships.** Continuous learning and self-improvement empower individuals to navigate life's challenges and seize opportunities.

Financial prosperity supports personal growth and relationship-building. **Financial stability and wealth provide the resources and security needed to pursue personal goals and nurture relationships.** Effective financial planning reduces stress and creates a sense of control over one's future. Financial prosperity also enables individuals to give back and support others.

Meaningful relationships enrich personal development and financial prosperity. **Social connections provide emotional support, opportunities for growth, and a sense of belonging.** Building strong relationships enhances well-being and resilience. Collaborative efforts and networking can lead to new opportunities and financial success.

In conclusion, the synergy of personal development, financial prosperity, and relationships creates a harmonious and fulfilling life. **Investing in self-awareness, financial literacy, and relationship-building enhances overall well-being and prosperity.** Achieving harmony between these pillars empowers individuals to reach their full potential and live a prosperous life.

15

Chapter 15: The Journey to the Pinnacle of Unity

The journey to the pinnacle of unity is a lifelong pursuit of growth, prosperity, and connection. **Embracing this journey with an open heart and a curious mind is essential for achieving harmony and fulfillment.** This chapter encourages readers to embrace the journey and offers practical tips for continuous growth.

Continuous learning is a key aspect of the journey to unity. **Staying curious and open to new experiences enhances personal development and broadens perspectives.** Whether through formal education, reading, or exploring new hobbies, continuous learning keeps the mind engaged and fosters growth.

Adaptability is crucial for navigating the ever-changing landscape of life. **Being open to change and willing to adapt to new circumstances enhances resilience and the ability to thrive.** Embracing a growth mindset and viewing challenges as opportunities for learning support adaptability. Flexibility and a positive outlook enable individuals to navigate uncertainties with confidence.

Perseverance is essential for overcoming obstacles and achieving long-term goals. **Staying committed to personal development, financial planning, and relationship-building requires dedication and effort.** Recognizing that setbacks are part of the journey and maintaining a resilient mindset supports perseverance. Celebrating small successes along the way reinforces motivation and progress.

In conclusion, the journey to the pinnacle of unity is a lifelong pursuit of growth, prosperity, and connection. **Embracing continuous learning, adaptability, and perseverance enhances overall well-being and fulfillment.** The journey to unity empowers individuals to achieve harmony and live a prosperous and balanced life.

Book Description: The Pinnacle of Unity: Fusing Personal Development with Financial and Relational Prosperity

In the intricate dance of life, true success comes from harmonizing personal growth, financial stability, and meaningful relationships. "The Pinnacle of Unity" is your guide to achieving this balance, leading you to a prosperous and fulfilling life.

Discover the Foundation of Self-Awareness: Learn the essential techniques to understand yourself deeply, unlocking the keys to personal development and setting the stage for holistic growth.

Master the Art of Goal Setting: Transform your dreams into achievable milestones with SMART goals and actionable roadmaps, ensuring motivation and progress every step of the way.

Embrace a Growth Mindset: Overcome challenges with resilience and adaptability, viewing obstacles as opportunities for learning and growth.

Achieve Financial Prosperity: Gain financial literacy and discover smart investing strategies, building wealth and securing your financial future.

Cultivate Meaningful Relationships: Strengthen family bonds, expand your social network, and enhance emotional intelligence to create a supportive and connected community.

Achieve Work-Life Balance: Implement effective strategies to manage time and energy, ensuring harmony between work and personal life.

Foster Gratitude and Positivity: Cultivate a positive mindset and practice gratitude to enhance well-being and resilience.

Experience the Synergy of Unity: Understand how personal development, financial prosperity, and relationships are interconnected, and learn to

CHAPTER 15: THE JOURNEY TO THE PINNACLE OF UNITY

integrate these pillars for a harmonious life.

Embark on a Lifelong Journey: Embrace continuous learning, adaptability, and perseverance, guiding you toward the pinnacle of unity and prosperity.

"The Pinnacle of Unity" offers a comprehensive and practical guide to achieving a harmonious and fulfilling life. Whether you're seeking personal growth, financial stability, or stronger relationships, this book provides the insights and tools to help you reach the pinnacle of unity, where all aspects of life come together in a prosperous and balanced symphony.

www.ingramcontent.com/pod-product-compliance
Lightning Source LLC
LaVergne TN
LVHW020503080526
838202LV00057B/6128